THE
POWER
OF
RESPONSIBILITY

Six Decisions To
Take Back Happiness And
Create Unlimited Success

JOELLE CASTEIX

DEDICATION

For Nick
May you always have the world on a string.

TABLE OF CONTENTS

INTRODUCTION

> *It doesn't matter who you were yesterday. It doesn't matter who you were five minutes ago. The only things that matter are who you are right now and the kind of person you decide to be from this moment onward.*

Bankrupt businesses, broken marriages, destroyed relationships, rising debt, bad luck, lousy careers—failures surround us. And it seems like no matter what we do, some of us will never break this cycle ...

Unless you read this book.

Before we begin, I want you to do something drastic: put aside every other self-help or business book you own.

Yes, it sounds crazy, but bear with me. Whether the books you're reading are about finding wealth, flipping houses, succeeding in your career, doing well in college, finding inner peace, making money on the Internet, or coping with addiction, these books are USELESS without the tools I am going to give you.

Before any of these books work, there is something you have to do first.

It's not the fault of the other books or the authors that they missed this first key step.

The rest of their information most likely is invaluable. However, unless you know how to flip your switch, those books—or any self-help program—will never work. You have to be READY to succeed, and you can't do that if your switch is stuck on off.

That switch is responsibility. And it will change your life.

* * *

Look around you. We live in a world where people don't know how to be happy.

How many times have you said to yourself, "I'll never lose the weight." "I'll never get that job." "I'll never get ahead. I'll never win." "I hate the holidays." "I'm stuck living paycheck to paycheck." "Why does everyone else get the lucky breaks?" ... and on, and on, and on.

How many times have you listened to your friends and colleagues complain about their marriages, children, friends, careers, or future?

We spend millions of dollars on self-help books, but they sit on our shelves, collecting dust. Or we read them over and over again, but after a while, we begin to think that they might work only for the chosen few. We get deeper and deeper into debt, even though wonderful financial tools are available to us. We are unhappy, even though tools to help us be happy abound. Many of our relationships fail, even though our partner, child, friend, or spouse wants to make things work. Why?

2

For most people, self-help books and courses will NEVER work.

Because they lack ONE simple tool.

What if I told you that I had a magic, fool-proof formula that could instantly change your life for the better and give you unlimited potential for happiness and success? What if I told you that the formula was easy and almost painless?

Would you listen?

* * *

I am an expert in responsibility. My TEDx talk on the subject went viral.

I have helped people as diverse as childhood sexual abuse survivors and business leaders, entrepreneurs and college students change their lives with the strategies I will share with you. I will show you how to turn your biggest liability—victimhood—into your biggest asset: responsibility. I have shown people how to turn around negative thinking, be receptive to change, act as true listeners, and—most importantly—how to become engaged in life.

Being positive and powerful is a choice. I'm going to show you how to make it.

Taking responsibility is a 180-degree life decision. Reading this book and using my simple tools will help you take control of your career. You can rebuild damaged relationships on a safe, solid foundation. You will finally be able to let go of the toxic people in your life—and do so in a healthy way. If you are an enabler, following the tools and steps in this book will help you create strong boundaries. You can let go of co-dependency and stop hurting the people you love. By taking responsibility, you will make not only yourself but also those you enable become stronger.

If you are building a business or starting out on your own, responsibility is the tool that will take you from an average business owner to a superstar in your industry. When you realize that you are in complete control of your success and your future, your competitors—who will not have these tools—won't stand a chance.

Thought leaders in business have been beating the responsibility drum for decades. Former Dean of the Stanford Graduate School of Business Robert L. Joss said, "Too many leaders get caught up in thinking about power rather than their responsibility to those they lead."

J.K. Rowling, whose stratospheric success is a direct result of the power of personal responsibility, said, "There is an expiry date on blaming your parents for steering you in the wrong direction. The moment you are old enough to take the wheel, responsibility lies with you."

Even Anne Frank, whose story of resilience and tragedy has influenced generations of young readers, writes in her diary, "Parents can only give good advice or put them on the right paths, but the final forming of a person's character lies in their own hands."

Researcher and storyteller Brene Brown says it best, "If you own this story, you get to write the ending."

Think about that for a moment: if you own your story, you get to write the ending. That's incredible. If given the chance, no one will write the story of his life with a sad, depressing ending. No one wants her legacy to be poverty, sadness, alienation, loss, or depression.

You CAN write your own ending, and it starts with a simple decision. All you need to do is flip the switch, and you can have a life that exceeds your dreams. Yes, you can open the door to wealth and success. And you will definitely also open the door to the one thing that is so elusive to so many people: authentic happiness.

Don't pass up on what everyone from business leaders to writers and storytellers say is the key to their continuing and increasing success.

It is in your power.

I am offering you a golden ticket. These proven methods will help you write your own ending, find authentic happiness, and develop unlimited potential. As an added bonus, I am also giving you the power to be able to accomplish anything and everything you want.

But if you stop reading here, you will miss out on the most amazing, fulfilling journey of your life.

I refuse to be a statistic. You don't have to be one, either.

So turn the page, and let's get started.

CHAPTER ONE

WHY A BOOK ABOUT RESPONSIBILITY

In 2015, I gave a TEDx talk about a topic very close to my heart: responsibility. For me, responsibility is more than teaching children to do their chores or fulfilling my job obligations.

Responsibility is the greatest gift you can give yourself. It's the one thing that can help you realize your potential. It can help you map your way to unlimited success, encourage you to build wealth, allow you to create strong, loving relationships, and give you the ability the make the world a better place. With it, you can achieve ANYTHING.

It can do something even more important than anything else listed here: responsibility can save your life.

I am proof of that.

I am a survivor of child sexual abuse. From age 15 to 17, I was sexually abused by one of my high school teachers. Like many victims of this kind of abuse, I was carefully groomed. Predatory grooming is how a child-sex predator manipulates an especially vulnerable child with flattery, time, gifts, and attention. It's how a predator can blur sexual boundaries and create a victim who is compliant—that is, one who is too confused and scared to fight back. I was a typical vulnerable victim—I came from a home with an alcoholic mother and a father in a deep sense of denial.

By the time the abuse was over, I was 17 and pregnant, had a sexually transmitted disease, and was utterly alone. The man who abused me was a master at manipulation, so I had no support system.

In fact, my friends and parents blamed me for the abuse.

It was not a time I ever want to revisit.

If you are familiar with the after-effects of this kind of abuse, you know that survivors suffer from horrible shame and self-loathing. Many are so psychologically injured by the abuse that they take their own lives. Others, who might not be suicidal, start down a track of self-destruction. Whether by choice or fate, these survivors end up in situations where victimhood becomes the norm. For me, I took the road of bad relationships, depression, isolation, self-hatred, and always finding myself at the wrong place at the wrong time.

I only knew how to be a victim.

By the time I was 27, I was divorced, living at home with my father, jobless, clinically depressed, intermittently suicidal, and facing a future with little potential. Looking back on my past, I saw only shame and embarrassment. The future I mapped for myself—if I stayed on this course—was bleak.

But then something happened. I looked around and realized that my life didn't have to be this way.

I don't know why it happened or why my eyes opened. At that moment, however, I clearly saw that I could change my life if I made a commitment to myself.

It was shocking.

At that moment, I realized that I had a choice: I could live, or I could die. If I stayed on this life trajectory, I was going to die.

Bad luck and poor decisions had begotten more bad luck and more poor decisions. I was miserable. And the reason I was staying miserable was because—I thought—I didn't know how to be any other way. Suicide or self-destruction would eventually win.

I didn't want to die. However, if things didn't change, I had a one-way, express ticket to my own funeral.

That wasn't what I wanted anymore.

I wanted to live. No, I wanted to THRIVE. I wanted to be truly happy. But how could I accomplish that?

I began to think. I had spent years blaming my abuser, peers, and parents for my misery. I blamed fate because I always seemed to be in bad situations. I blamed myself for falling into bad relationships and badly treating people I cared about. I blamed everybody, especially myself, for my depression.

I saw a pattern.

I had made a career of pointing fingers and placing blame. That's what victims do.

But I had done nothing to make a change. I had done nothing to get myself out of this rut. But what if the true power to change was in me all along? What if the missing link to happiness and success was ... me?

It wasn't until I put down my pointing fingers that I realized that I had had the formula for happiness all along. It was my *Wizard of Oz* moment, but I couldn't find happiness and success by simply clicking my heels and going home. I had to do something difficult.

If I wanted to live and thrive, I had to take responsibility. I had to take responsibility for my life ... my future ... and my past. It was a big pill to swallow, but anything was better—and easier—than how I was living.

The first promise to myself was the biggie.

I had to take responsibility for the fact that yes, my abuse had happened. I couldn't change it. It was there, and I had to deal with it.

I'm not talking about blame here. I'm talking about responsibility. It was not my fault that I was abused, but dwelling on the pain and blaming other people for my circumstances did nothing to help me heal. If I kept looking back, I could never move forward.

That's when I realized something. By taking responsibility for the fact that my abuse had happened, I gave myself permission to take responsibility for my healing and my future.

By taking responsibility, I took back control of my life.

However, it didn't end there.

By taking responsibility, I had to own the fact that my life since the abuse was a direct result of decisions I had made. Nobody else made those decisions for me. No one else pushed me on my path.

I built that path of shame, self-destruction, and victimhood all by myself.

Oh no! Then I realized that I couldn't blame my parents anymore! In fact, once I became objective about my life, I realized that my parents did a pretty darned good job of raising me. I graduated from college, and I was a high-achieving student. I was a good person with a strong work ethic, solid values, and great friendships made in college and afterward. I had good parents.

It was time to stop blaming them for everything.

Thinking about blame and my high-school peers conjured up a whole different barrel full of emotions. Why? I had to stop blaming them, too.

When I put on my objective thinker cap and really looked back at what had happened in high school, I could see why my friends were so hurt and angry. We were all children when my abuse happened. (Take a look at a bunch of 15-year-olds, and tell me if you think they can handle the scope and scale of a child-sex abuse scandal).

They were collateral damage—my abuser threatened them, alienated them, and threw them into a world where they did not belong. School administrators who should have been superheroes turned their backs. In a way, my classmates were just as hurt and betrayed as I was. A child predator groomed and used them to gain sexual access to one of their friends. Of course, they were going to be hurt and angry. I finally understood and appreciated their anger. It wasn't their fault. It wasn't my fault.

11

But I had to take responsibility for the circumstances surrounding my abuse. By doing that, I could own my story and tell my friends how truly sorry I was that they were hurt, even though it was not my fault. If they chose to not accept my apology, I could hold my head up high. Their feelings were their responsibility, not mine.

I was no longer a victim. I had regained my power and could change my life.

My abuser would never see a day behind bars for what he did to me because the criminal statute of limitations had expired. However, I could use the civil courts to expose him and the cover-up at my high school. I was able to gain and make public my abuser's signed confession stating that he abused me and numerous other girls. By taking responsibility and seeking accountability through the court system, I could expose him and warn the community of the threat he posed. Had I still been living in a victim mentality, I never would have been able to seize that opportunity.

I was amazed to watch as taking responsibility grew into something larger than myself. By standing up in civil court, I could keep other children safe, hold my abuser accountable, and begin to fight for justice for other people. For the first time, I had a purpose bigger than myself. I found dignity. I found authentic pride. I found that I could be happy. I was able to realize that the future was as bright as I wanted to make it. I didn't have to be a victim anymore.

I was in the driver's seat, so to speak. If I could take responsibility for my abuse and how I had lived my life, I could also wake up every morning and make the decision to be happy. I could make the decision to be successful. I could make the decision to fill my life with love, get rid of toxic people and ideas, and go to bed with a smile on my face.

The only person who could make me happy and create my success was myself. No self-help book or therapist could make me happy or give me answers if I didn't make the true, conscious decision to help myself first.

That true, conscious decision is responsibility.

Since I made the decision to take responsibility, my life has been a rocket-ship ride. I have become a worldwide advocate and spokesperson for survivors of sexual abuse. My book on abuse prevention for parents is a bestseller. I am an in-demand speaker, using my experience to inspire people to achieve anything they want. I have traveled the world, spreading the word about responsibility and abuse prevention, helping survivors, and motivating people to change their lives.

The ride gets better every day, and what I am most proud of is my family. Before I took responsibility for my happiness and future, I thought that I could never be a good mother. I was convinced that I could never be a good wife. I believed that I would always be alone. Now, I spend every day celebrating a dynamic marriage. Sure, we argue and disagree, but we have made the decision to embrace and challenge each other to become better individuals.

Every day I spend with my son is a joy. Sure, he tries my patience and plays too many videogames (and forgets to take a bath far more often than he remembers), but he is the culmination of everything I have ever done that is good. He is the direct product of my decision to take responsibility. He is beautiful—even if my husband and I lose everything tomorrow, we will look at him and consider ourselves to be the most blessed people we know.

If I can do it, so can you.

After my TEDx talk went online, I was blown away by the positive response. The video went viral overnight. People I had never met told me that my words had saved their lives—and I'm not only talking about survivors of sexual abuse.

Business owners have written to tell me that they could turn around their businesses. Teachers told me that they started to enjoy their jobs again because they took responsibility for their happiness. My own father, with whom I now have a wonderful relationship, told me that aging and hearing loss were making him depressed ... and aging him even faster. When he made the decision to take responsibility for his happiness, though, he found solutions falling into his lap. He called it luck.

However, he didn't become lucky. Instead, by taking responsibility, he could finally grasp all the wonderful opportunities to which he had been blind. Once the dark cloud of negativity, blame, and victimhood was lifted, a world of happiness was finally visible.

You have the power to do and achieve anything you want.
Let's begin the journey.

CHAPTER TWO

RESPONSIBILITY:
GEORGE WASHINGTON AND THE MYTH THAT FORMED THE MAN

When I was a child, the first lesson we learned in school about George Washington wasn't about the Revolutionary War, his presidency, or his lasting legacy at Mount Vernon.

We learned about the cherry tree.

If you don't know the story, it goes something like this: George Washington was walking around his family's orchard with his new, favorite hatchet. As George walked up and down the rows of trees, he admired the hatchet's sharp, shiny blade and thought about all the amazing things he could build with the wood he could harvest with it. In a corner of the orchard stood a cherry tree. It wasn't a big tree, so young George knew that it wouldn't take him long to chop it down. It didn't take many hatchet swings before the tree was on the ground.

George's excitement was immediately followed by dread. He remembered that his father had warned him against chopping down trees. The elder Washington had given the boy the hatchet with a stern warning: Don't destroy trees that can give us beautiful things while they are still alive. George looked down at the tree. Now, he saw that the sapling was actually quite young and had been chopped down long before it had the opportunity to give the family years of cherry harvests.

George ran home and hid.

Later that day, the elder Washington walked to the grove to check on his trees. There was a young tree that needed special care. Washington had spent time carefully grafting new experimental growths onto the tree and wanted to see how the fragile sapling was doing. When he got to where the tree had been growing, he discovered that someone had chopped it down.

The elder Washington went home, sure of the culprit. When he got to the house, he found his son George hiding with his nose behind a book. "Did you cut down the cherry tree?" his father asked.

The boy put down the book he was reading and picked up his prized new hatchet.

"I cannot tell a lie, father," the boy said. "It was I who cut down the cherry tree."

"I understand, my son," his father said. "In telling me the truth, you have become a man." And for schoolchildren everywhere, a legend was born (although we never learned if George lost his hatchet privileges).

Now, if you were to stand in a room full of historians, every one of them would say the same thing: that story is pure myth. There is no evidence that anything like the "Washington Cutting down the Cherry Tree" story ever happened. The whole yarn is a figment of someone's imagination.

But why do we love this particular myth so much? Why are there still children's books, cartoons, and songs about a story that doesn't have a grain of truth?

It's because the story teaches us about responsibility.

Why is it important that someone like George Washington has this trait? As Robert L. Joss said in the introduction, true leadership does not come from power but from responsibility.

There is no trait more admired in leaders, friends, significant others, business partners, and children than responsibility. It is the trait that helps us build and create trust, unleash our potential, create authentic self-esteem, and find true happiness that is not blinded by fear, paranoia, secrets, or self-doubt.

But what is responsibility actually?

Responsibility by Definition

Dictionary.com defines responsibility as "the state or fact of being responsible, answerable, or accountable for something within one's power, control, or management."

There is a lot in this short definition.

First, let's talk about what responsibility isn't. Responsibility is NOT blame. Although we tend to use the terms interchangeably, blame and responsibility are very different. Let's turn again to Dictionary. com, which defines blame as "find fault with; censure."

On one hand, blame is a reprimand. It's a punishment. Blame is something imposed (by another person or oneself) in reaction to a hurtful action. Blame implies a need for contrition or shame.

Responsibility, on the other hand, is a gift that we can only find within ourselves. At times, it might involve contrition—the act of being sorry and making amends—but it does not involve shame or punitive punishment. It's empowerment, as opposed to a penalty.

In my TEDx talk about responsibility, I discuss the destructive power of blame. It's what people do when they are angry, scared, or confused or can't understand why something horrible has happened.

I know that firsthand. As I began to disclose to my parents and peers that I had been sexually abused as a child, they were quick to blame me for the abuse. Why? They were hurt, scared, and confused and didn't understand anything about child-sex abuse. They had been carefully groomed by my abuser and led to believe that he was so beyond reproach that it had to have been my fault that these bad things happened.

When it came to my parents, blame was an obvious choice. By blaming me, they didn't have to look closely at the poor circumstances in our home that could have contributed to my vulnerability. If they didn't point the finger of blame at me, they would have to assume the responsibility themselves.

Everyone was busy pointing fingers and placing blame on everyone else EXCEPT for the person who was truly responsible: the man who sexually abused me.

20

The effect on me was terrible.

It worked—I was in such a state of weakness and vulnerability that I allowed myself to absorb their accusations and blame. In no time at all, I began to truly believe what they were telling me: I was the wrongdoer. I was a 15 year old who had seduced an adult. I was the reason that he went on to sexually abuse other girls.

From the seed of blame grew shame.

I let blame and shame consume me. And they almost destroyed me.

Blame is an ugly force of nature. It's why innocent women were accused of being witches and burned in Salem. It's why despondent men and women commit suicide. It's the reason we have wars. Blame is what wrecks families and relationships. Blame, wrongly placed, can destroy lives.

Shame is even more pernicious. Unlike guilt, which is about an action (think: *I have done a bad thing*), shame defines people and who they believe they are (think: *I am a bad person*). People guilty of crimes serve jail terms. People with shame give themselves a life sentence.

In my case, I carried blame and shame like a 1,000-pound bag of rocks. They were a weight that I thought I could never shed. As long as I held them, I could never stand up straight. I could never grow. I could never hug someone else with love and authenticity because the blame and shame told me that I was flawed and wrong.

21

Soon, I didn't want to let go. Blame and shame became part of my identity. They were things on which I could count. They were friends who would never abandon me. Shame told me I was a bad person. Blame reinforced it. And I rationalized it like this: at least I knew who I was and that I was unworthy. I called it honesty. All the while, blame and shame were destroying me—and they were lies.

Let's go back to that day of clarity when I finally understood that I had a choice. One of the realizations I made was that self-blame and shame were not making me any better. They were not helping me heal. I was not helping other people. Instead, blame and shame were killing me. If I kept blaming myself, I would die.

That was the day that I decided to put down that 1,000-pound bag.

My healing was a long process, but the first thing I had to do was stop mixing up the terms "blame" and "responsibility." It was a watershed moment for me. I could take responsibility for the fact that my abuse happened, but I didn't have to blame myself for it. I didn't have to place value judgments on myself or curse myself. Even more importantly, I didn't have to let anyone else curse me or place value judgments on me anymore. I didn't have to embrace shame.

With blame and shame, there is no redemption. There is no happy ending after someone is told, "It's all your fault." We no longer think, "I did something wrong."

We think, "I AM something wrong."

When blame and shame are in the picture, we lose the power to write our own ending. Why? Blame and shame are a trap. They are a trap based on lies.

When you place blame and find fault in yourself, you take away your power to be accountable. You take away any potential you have to create real, positive change.

To put it simply, blame and shame are things that we try to escape.

This book is not about escaping. It's about thriving. That's where responsibility comes in.

Let's go back to the George Washington myth.

Mythical stories are powerful. They teach us our most important life lessons. By taking difficult subjects and turning them into simple children's myths and stories, we make these lessons easy to remember and accessible to a wide audience.

Just think about how myths make things easy to remember. We remember the story of George Washington and the cherry tree or of the tortoise and the hare, but how many of us know off the top of our heads who the 22nd president of the United States was? (Don't worry; I looked it up for you. It was Grover Cleveland.)

If the power of responsibility is important enough to get its own myth (with the father of our country as the star), there must be something to it, don't you think?

When I was a child, I wondered why George didn't get into more trouble and why his father was so quick to forgive when George admitted that he had, indeed, hacked his father's prized tree into kindling. But as I grew older, I began to see the wisdom.

By accepting responsibility, young George was able to be accountable. Yes, he was scared, but he didn't accept shame. And because he didn't lie or make excuses, he didn't build the sandy foundation of deceit that would always shift under him.

Now that we have a definition of responsibility—and a celebrated myth to help us better understand it—what can responsibility do in our lives? What does it mean for you, sitting here, reading this book?

What does the responsible person look like? How can you change the way you work, relate to your family, build your business, or create your future?

How can the failure to take responsibility destroy not only *your* credibility but also corporations and nations?

How can you use responsibility to create your unlimited potential and write your own ending?

We'll start unlocking the clues in the next chapter.

CHAPTER THREE

THE RESPONSIBLE PERSON

Life is a series of failures, but the responsible person is the one who realizes that failure is the seed from which authentic success blossoms.

In colonial America, people didn't have much choice about accepting responsibility. If you wanted to eat, stay warm in the winter, provide for your family, have a roof over your head, and be accepted in the community, you had to take responsibility.

There was no second option. There were no safety nets. If you wanted to survive, you had to take responsibility for yourself and the people who depended on you. Other people could—maybe—help you out in times of need, but if you continually refused to take responsibility for yourself or your family, you faced hunger, homelessness, and death.

We, though, are in the 21st century. We are surrounded by choices. Safety nets—some good, some bad—are the norm. It becomes easy to mistake someone who is simply getting by with someone who is responsible and successful.

If you are going to embrace the power of responsibility, you need to know what responsible people look like. You need to know who they are to learn and adopt the attributes and decisions that allow them to succeed and thrive.

How does the responsible person look. speak, act, and react today? What makes this person happier and more successful and gives this person far more potential than the average Joe?

Here's a hint: responsible people look just like you do, but they are smiling on the inside. Let's figure out why.

Traits of Responsible People

Responsible people know when to seek help and how to ask for it. If there are moments when responsible people feel hopeless, they stop, take a deep breath, and understand that help is there for the asking.

The result: the responsible person asks for and gets help and succeeds.

Responsible people know that their emotions are in their control and should not be used to manipulate other people. Responsible people are not enablers. They understand that, if they demand to be treated with kid gloves, they cannot embrace their personal power and succeed. They also know that, if they rely solely on others to carry them emotionally through life, they hurt themselves, as well as the people who help them.

The responsible person sheds toxic relationships and instead attracts people who embrace positivity.

Responsible people know that emotions are powerful and should be respected but also that emotions should not be used hurt, manipulate, or control other people (think: "Oh no, don't upset Joelle. She will ruin the entire holiday if you ask her about her health/politics/religion. And never disagree with her. She will never let you forget it.")

They do not dwell on the past but learn from the lessons of the past. A responsible person understands that dwelling on the past will not help anyone and that focusing on past mistakes won't ensure that they will not be repeated. They don't use the bad facts of their past to manipulate or shame other people—or themselves.

They give themselves permission. They are kind to themselves. We tend to deny ourselves things (either consciously or unconsciously) because we think that we don't deserve them.

We deny ourselves permission to be healthy when we constantly cheat on our diets or don't make time for exercise. We deny ourselves permission to do well at work when we act in ways we know are detrimental to our careers.

We deny ourselves permission to take responsibility when we fall back into victim-like behaviors.

When responsible people fall into these traps, they tell themselves, "I give myself permission to be happy/responsible/successful."

These are mighty, powerful words. Responsible people use them every day.

Responsible people are compassionate toward the people who need it the most: themselves.

They admit and apologize for mistakes and make amends for any harm. The responsible person knows that denying or covering up mistakes is cowardly and will only lead to more problems.

The responsible person knows that owning mistakes and treating them like life lessons is empowering. Embracing mistakes as lessons takes away other people's ability to use guilt, shame, or other punitive measures. When the responsible person treats mistakes as life lessons, they can no longer be used as weapons of self-destruction or shame.

The responsible person knows that owning mistakes is the key to becoming an innovative, positive change agent.

Responsible people understand the importance of integrity and promises. When they say they will do something, it gets done. If, for some reason, they can't deliver, they explain why and work on a solution.

Responsible people don't dodge accountability.

They also don't blame other people or circumstances. ("It's his fault I missed this deadline." "If I had good instructions, I would have gotten this done." "No one else meets deadlines. Why should I?") Responsible people can encourage, guide, teach, empower, and help themselves and other people. They don't make excuses for poor behavior or outcomes.

Responsible people separate morality from goals. I'll admit that this one was huge for me. I am a perfectionist, and let me tell you, being a perfectionist is not easy. I was the child who cried if I colored outside the lines, beat myself up if I got a B, felt ashamed if I got in trouble, and considered myself a failure if I didn't meet a goal.

Why did I do things like this to myself? I equated my self-worth—whether I was a morally good person—with my achievements.

Responsible people don't do that.

Why? Because they know that failure is the first step to success. They know that not all goals are met the first time. If they fail, they are just motivated to try again—feeling stronger for learning from their mistakes. They let go of perfectionism and realize that their worth is in who they are, not what they achieve.

The responsible student understands that education is a system. To get good grades and succeed, responsible people know that they have to understand their professor, do the required work, and ask for help if they fail a test or get a poor grade. Responsible students don't beg or demean teachers into changing grades but, instead, do the work to get the best grade they can.

They seek solutions instead of complaining. Nobody enjoys a complainer. No one enjoys the person who never helps but always criticizes.

There is a complainer in every workplace and every family: the person who complains about everything from the temperature to the Thanksgiving turkey. The complainer never offers to help or suggests a solution but always brings other people down. To the complainer, the world—school, work, home—is unfair and unchanging.

Responsible people might complain once, and then they take action and work to find a solution. Why? No one becomes successful or happy when all he does is complain and focus on the negative.

Responsible people understand the difference between following instructions and ethical decision-making. You might have heard of the Enron scandal, which destroyed an entire company (and the retirement savings of thousands of people). You might have also heard of the sex abuse scandals in Penn State University, the Boy Scouts, and the Catholic Church. These organizations weren't full of bad people who wanted to cover up crimes and abuse.

In fact, the opposite was true. These organizations were full of good people who followed instructions, refused to ask questions, passed the buck, or turned a blind eye to wrongdoing. They expected other people to do the right (and difficult) thing.

Responsible people stand up for what is morally and ethically right, even if they know that they will hit resistance.

Had at least one responsible person stood up at Enron, the company might still be in business today. How many children could have been saved from abuse had an administrator in the Boy Scouts or the Catholic Church called the police when that person knew that a crime had been committed?

Responsible people don't use shame to force others to change. Truly responsible people know that, to motivate others to succeed, everyone must be treated with respect. Using shame, guilt, or unprofessional behavior (yelling, screaming) accomplishes nothing, except to engender fear, rage, or the desire for retribution.

Responsible people also know that they cannot change other people or have power over them. They, however, can use positive influences to help others take better paths. If other people do not want to change, the responsible person knows when to walk away.

They evaluate people on their character and merits. Martin Luther King said it best in his "I Have a Dream" speech. Responsible people do not judge others (positively or negatively) solely on their skin color, wealth, religion, position, or sphere of influence. Instead, the responsible person evaluates others based on their merits, character, and morality.

Responsible people embrace accountability. Deadlines? They like them. Accolades? They love them. Constructive criticism? They embrace it. Being held accountable? They would have it no other way. They take ownership of projects and promises.

Responsible people celebrate success and work through challenges. They also realize that authentic self-esteem comes from achievement. Whether that achievement is winning a race, working hard in school, meeting a tough deadline, or having a strong marriage, authentic self-esteem comes from knowing that one is good and capable and embraces opportunity with love.

Responsible people know how to shut down bad self-talk. We all know how this goes. Everything is fine and dandy until that little voice inside our head says, "You always mess stuff up." "You're a failure." "You're no good." "You should be ashamed."

Responsible people know how to minimize the importance of this voice and eventually shut it down.

Stopping the negative messages in our head takes time and habit, but responsible people know that they have nothing but time.

Responsible people take steps to take care of themselves. They know that they are no one's savior but have a responsibility to themselves for their own health, happiness, and energy.

You can't be responsible and accountable if you are sick and tired and doing too much for other people.
The responsible person manages stress and gets enough sleep. The responsible person knows how to manage time.

Responsible people know how to say "no." Too many of us are scared to say "no" when asked to give time, money, goods, or services. As a result, we are spread too thin and cannot be the people we need to be for our families and ourselves. Responsible people understand the liberating power of the word "no."

They don't feel like they always have to please other people by spreading themselves too thin. They know the difference between going above and beyond and overdoing it at the expense of themselves and the people they love.

Responsible people know that saying "no" might hurt feelings, but they explain why it is the appropriate, healthy, and right answer. If other people remain hurt, responsible people apologize and refuse to be manipulated into changing course.

We know what responsible people look like and how they interact with other people—now what? How do you become a responsible person?

You've learned about focus. You learned about George Washington. You know the definition of responsibility and how it differs from shame and blame.

Now, it's time to check your focus.

CHAPTER FOUR

ESCAPING THE TRAP OF VICTIMHOOD OR WHERE YOU LOOK IS WHERE YOU GO

Responsibility is a lesson in focus.

My son is a typical child: if there is a car, bike, or board that goes somewhere, he wants to drive it, ride it, steer it, and push it to its limits. He is 9 years old, and we have seen more than our share of accidents and mishaps.

Last year, he was invited to a go-kart track. These high-speed cars were fast on the track and made children's hearts race. After the safety presentation, my son and his buddies strapped on safety gear and buckled themselves into their kart of choice.
Before they blazed off at record speeds, I remembered a lesson I received in driver's education. I was 16 and taking a behind-the-wheel driving class.

After a near-miss in traffic, my instructor chastised me for looking at pedestrians on the sidewalk instead of the road. He told me that our brains are very powerful and will pull our bodies (and, in this case, the steering wheel) toward wherever we are looking.

"That's why I keep telling you to keep your eyes on the road," he said. "It's not nagging. It's science. Where you look is where you go. Keep your focus on the road."

Channeling my driver's education instructor, I shouted to my son over the safety wall, "Remember, where you look is where you go."

He gave me a confused look, shrugged, and slammed on the gas.

The first few laps were slow, but soon, the children began to get the hang of things. By the 10th lap, they were in the groove. They figured out how to steer through the curves, accelerate at the right moments, and not rely totally on their brake pedals. They each got a little faster and a little more daring. And faster. And faster.

Then it happened.

WHAM!

One of the boys spotted his mom on the sidelines. Proud of his driving, he waved and shouted at her, "Look, Mom! Look! See me, Mom? See?"

Then, before he could finish speaking, his kart slammed into the safety fence ... right in front of where his mother was standing and holding her youngest child.

We all got a shock, but no one was hurt. The safety fence was strong, and the go-kart was sturdy. The boy laughed at his crash, turned the steering wheel, and re-entered the go-kart race with his friends. His mother, though, had to sit down for a few minutes.

On the drive home, I asked my son if he had seen the crash.

"Yeah, Mom, it was awesome." he told me. "He slammed right into the wall where his mom was. I was right behind him. I don't know why he decided to turn into the wall like that, but it was cool."

My inner driving instructor came to the surface.

"He didn't decide to turn toward the wall," I told him. "Did you hear what I shouted at you right before you started racing?"

My son thought for a moment. "Yeah," he said. "You said, 'Where you look is where you go.'" He paused.

"Oh, I get it."

And so should you.

The idea of "Where you look is where you go" applies to far more than go-karts and my parents' 1985 Toyota. My driving instructor was right: the brain is a very powerful organ. It can overtake your intentions—no matter how admirable—and take you in an entirely opposite direction. As in the incident with the go-kart, your brain will take you where your eyes lead you.

I'm not talking only about your physical eyes. I'm also talking about your attitude and your state of mind. Where you look is where you go. If you are only looking at the past and focusing on the negative, that is where your brain will take you.

Really. Where you look is where you go.

If you spend your time thinking about your past, that's where your brain will take you. If you are consumed with your mistakes, challenges, losses, and the places where you are lacking ... guess what? That is where your brain will take you.

That's why we remain victims. It's a matter of misplaced focus.

If all you can see is what you lack, your failures and pain, the mistakes of your past, and your loss, depression, and fear, that is where your brain will take your body, and that is where your life will stay.

Why do you think that some people—who have no balance or mobility issues—are more accident prone than others? Why are some people always unlucky or regularly in the wrong place at the wrong time? It's because their negative focus unconsciously leads them there.

We all have coworkers who are tough to be around. The person who is full of aches and pains. Her car is kaput, and her rent is going up. The boss is out to get him, and he can't seem to shake this constant cough. When you ask this person about his family, he tells you that his home is horrible and only getting worse. His children are disrespectful, he will never be able to afford their college tuition, and they're on their way to becoming a bunch of bums. You've learned to never ask this person about work. She tells you that work projects are stupid and a chore. In fact, she continually complains that, if management just listened to her, everything would be better.

This person is miserable to be around. It's even more miserable to be this person. No one likes her, and no one wants to work with him. Of course, managers avoid this person like the plague.

These people—full of negativity, spite, anger, depression, poor self-talk, and fear—have created a world where they are permanent victims. Their negativity destroys every aspect of their lives.

They say that nothing is their fault, even though these are a world and an attitude that they have created.

And they are the only ones who don't see it.

However, there is usually another kind of person at work, too. One who is completely different. This is the positive person who always seems to win, be surrounded by love, have a successful career, and enjoy a life full of family. This is the person who is quick with a smile, helping hand, and good advice. This is the person who loves a good work or personal challenge. When this person isn't at work, he's coaching his children, learning a new skill, engrossed in a hobby, volunteering, or running races. Where she is and whatever she does, she's a people magnet. Usually, we say this person has it all.

What if having it all is not a matter of skill, education, or luck? What if it's about being responsible and positive? What if it's about making the decision to be happy, fulfilled, and successful?

What if I told you it's about your focus?

Whether entrepreneurs or employees of a larger business, successful people share one common attribute: they look to the future to create change and success.

That's not to say that we should ignore the mistakes of the past. Philosopher and poet George Santayana was right when he said, "those who cannot remember the past are condemned to repeat it."

However, to take responsibility, you will have to refine your focus.

Of course, I remember my past and the mistakes I have made. Of course, I remember the times when I didn't take responsibility. I also remember that I do not want to go back there, so I have decided to take responsibility because if I continue to look back, that is where I will go. And I am not going back. I decided to focus on today and tomorrow. I decided to take responsibility. I decided to be happy.

I refined my focus.

Where you look is where you go.

And where you are going is totally in your control.

Experts in behavioral change say that it takes only 21 to 30 days to create a new habit. Take heart: the experts don't claim that these three to four weeks are easy. If you struggle and falter, it's okay.

The key is your focus. Where you look is where you go.

But first you have to shed your emotional crutches. What are emotional crutches? I discuss them in depth in the next chapter.

CHAPTER FIVE

OUR EMOTIONAL CRUTCHES AND WHY THEY HOLD US BACK

It's time to get rid of our emotional crutches once and for all.

What is an emotional crutch? It's on what we lean when we are sad, depressed, ashamed, or enabled.

We all know the use of physical crutches. If we break a leg, crutches allow us to get from point A to point B while our leg heals. Once the leg heals, crutches are no longer needed. (Many people who have physical impairments regularly use crutches because they provide increased mobility, speed, and access to the outdoors. However, we are looking at people who use crutches after they are no longer needed, so we focus on the broken leg analogy.)

When events that emotionally hurt us happen, an emotional crutch can be beneficial for the short period of time it takes us to get better. The problem starts when we lean on this crutch after we should have healed or when we decide that it is easier to remain in a state of hurt.

Just like using a physical crutch after a broken leg has healed, leaning on an emotional crutch instead of healing and taking responsibility only holds the user back.

This chapter is about finding the emotional crutches in your life and throwing them away for good.

I have spent 15 years working with adult survivors of childhood sexual abuse, and throughout it, I have seen a lot of emotional crutches. The vast majority of the survivors are hurt very badly— physically, psychologically, and spiritually. Their wounds are deep, and most are invisible.

They needed crutches to simply survive their pain and begin the healing process. Until they didn't.

The real problems began when these men and women continue to cling to their crutches that are no longer needed—when they refuse to take responsibility for their healing. Once this happens, the emotional crutches begin to cause more damage.

The survivors who truly heal are those who make the decision to take responsibility and find out exactly what their crutches are and how to stand tall and strong without them.

This doesn't mean, though, that the survivor is all alone. Although we all have the power to throw away our emotional crutches, we don't have to fight the battle of responsibility alone. Sometimes, the only way to shed a crutch is to realize that you have to ask for help.

What are some of these emotional crutches?

The most obvious ones are our addictions to things, such as alcohol, drugs, and food. We become addicted for one primary reason: our addiction helps us feel better for a while. We use these addictions to mask pain and bury our problems.

Then, the disadvantages begin to far outweigh the positive fe-elings. When the addictions take control—even if they are not yet full-blown addictions—we lose the abilities to chart our own cour-se, plan our future, engage in relationships, and understand and feel love (especially self-love). When our addictions take control, we hurt the ones who love us, but mostly, we hurt ourselves.

That's the definition of an emotional crutch. And it has to go if you are going to embrace responsibility and write your own ending.

If you have a problem with drugs, alcohol, food, or another ad-dictive substance or activity, get help right now. You cannot take responsibility for your life when you let a substance numb you, hurt your relationships, and potentially destroy your future.

It's okay to ask for help.

As I said, no one expects you to white-knuckle your way through overcoming addiction. In cases of addiction, the best way to throw away your crutch is to accept the hand of someone willing to help you beat that addiction. Taking responsibility means that you don't have to go it alone.

It also means that you accept help from someone who will hold you accountable, not someone who will enable you, feel sorry for you, or make excuses for your behavior. An enabler makes it easy for you to remain an addict. You do not need or want an enabler in your life.

Other emotional crutches that need immediate intervention are depression, anxiety, bipolar disorder, and other emotional, mental, and psychiatric problems. It might seem crass to call these serious psychiatric conditions emotional crutches, but they are treatable. Therefore, responsibility comes into play.

Modern science has made amazing advances in the treatment and management of psychiatric and emotional disorders. In addition, proven alternative therapies abound. Practitioners across the United States, Canada, Europe, Australia, and other countries successfully help patients with pharmaceuticals and proven treatments, such as Eye Movement Desensitization and Reprocessing (EMDR) therapy, hypnotherapy, group therapy, coaching, talk therapy, and meditation. There is help out there when you choose to accept it.

Having battled anxiety and depression, I can tell you how easy it is to make these disorders an emotional crutch and excuse for bad behavior. I became comfortable in my pain because after years of depression, I began to believe pain was the only thing that I understood and could rely on. I was not alone. In fact, pain and isolation become crutches because we know that they will not abandon us. Anxiety and other psychiatric issues become our friends because we know exactly what to expect.

It is a horrible way to live. Why do we do it? We fear how much it will hurt to get better or that we will never get better at all.

This is not the case. It is a fallacy we create because we think it's safe. In reality, though, this way of living is far more dangerous than getting help.

If you suffer from any of these emotional or psychiatric conditions, get help. Accept the help that is offered to you. Do not look at your current state and think that you are undeserving or hopeless. Depression and other conditions are not signs of a poor character, immorality, or weaknesses. Do not be ashamed to admit that you have a medical condition which needs help.

If you still feel ashamed about your mental health, treat your brain like the biological organ that it is. If you had a painful liver disorder, and a doctor told you that you needed to take medicine and undergo a therapy that would help you heal, end painful symptoms, and give you a chance of a pain-free life, would you feel ashamed? Would you refuse the medication because you thought that your liver problem was a moral failure? Would you refuse therapy because you believed that you could beat your liver condition by being emotionally strong? No, of course not. You would take the medicine, go to the therapy, and end up feeling better.

Give your brain the same respect and love that you would give your liver.

The only person who can take the first step to getting better is you. And you deserve to feel better.

Other emotional crutches are not as obvious as addictions or depression. What about people who seem addicted to bad decision-making, toxic relationships, self-destructive behavior, anger, or victimhood?

Take a look at the following behaviors. Are any of these familiar to you?

- Having a constant bad attitude

- Maintaining toxic friendships

- Believing that you are always treated unfairly

- Poor decision-making (Do you often look back and think, "Why did I do that when I knew it would turn out badly?")

- Engaging in self-defeating behaviors (for example, quitting jobs, hobbies, or projects right before success)

- Overreacting emotionally to situations (so much so that people stop telling you the truth out of fear that you will overreact and make situations worse)

- Fearing challenges

- Thinking that people (e.g., teachers, bosses, parents) are out to get you

- Saying "I can't" more often than "I will"

- Expecting other people to fix your problems

- Being an emotional vampire who expects your friends to fix your problems while you suck their emotions dry

- Being accident prone

- Getting sick or injured often

- Pushing away people who want to help you

All of these are emotional crutches. Let's take a deeper look at a few of them.

Toxic relationships can be a huge crutch, and it's easy to see why. Friendships are powerful influences on how we live our lives. Friends bring us up or pull us down. It's our duty to figure out what kind of friends are more beneficial and help us be happier and more successful—and people who make the world a better place.

If we surround ourselves with positive, loving, successful friends who celebrate our successes, find joy in our happiness, challenge us to be better people, and lend us strong, helping hands, we will find ourselves becoming like them: strong, positive, and successful. However, if we surround ourselves with people who are negative and always point out our flaws, we will begin to only see our flaws. If we include among our friends people who believe that they need to bring others down a notch, then our chances of rising up the ladder of success are limited.

If we surround ourselves with needy people who begrudge our successes yet expect us to pick up the emotional pieces of *their* lives, we won't be able to be happy—or help them find happiness. It's toxic—these people will poison us as much as they continue to poison themselves.

These toxic relationships are not limited to friendships. The toxic people in our lives might be family members who mistake cruel or poor behavior for good intentions. They might take advantage of us or treat us badly because we're family and have to take it. The toxic person in our life might be our partner or spouse. It might even be our adult children.

It might be impossible to shed all toxic relationships, but you can change the way that you allow these people to affect and interact with you. Shedding toxic friends, putting up strong boundaries so that other people can't tear you down, and refusing to absorb other peoples' negativity can be tough.

But the rewards are great, most importantly, our happiness and success. Toxic relationships are emotional crutches that do us no good.

The only person who can take responsibility for your relationships is you.

Do you have other behaviors on the list that you wish you could control or stop? Do you find yourself sabotaging your success? Do you fear success or engage in self-limiting talk? ("Oh, I could never do that." "No, that's impossible." "I'm not smart/educated/clever/ daring enough to do something like that.")

Are you your own worst enemy? (I confess that this one has been a lifetime challenge for me.) Is it easier to criticize and curse your-self than it is to tell yourself, "I love you?" Do you tell yourself that you're fat, ugly, dumb, worthless, or a failure? (C'mon, we all do it. It's okay to nod.)

Are you unlucky or accident prone, or do you think the world is unfair? Are these events truly accidental, or are they partly your own creation? Has your negative attitude or poor outlook been a key influence?

If you are in school, does it seem like your teachers and professors are unfair to you? Do you feel like they are out to get you? Do you not get the grades you know you could earn because you think and act like a victim of your teachers?

These are all emotional crutches, and you have the power to change them.

The good news is that, with a little bit of practice, we can toss aside most of our emotional crutches. You understand your focus and the snare of victimhood. You are beginning to recognize what a responsible person looks like.

Now, it's time for some decision-making.

CHAPTER SIX

THE FIVE DECISIONS
THAT WILL CHANGE YOUR LIFE

Luck has nothing to do with your power to change.

I repeat: Luck has nothing to do with your success, happiness, or potential.

George Washington was not an outlier. Yes, he was the father of our country and the general who rallied our Revolutionary troops to an almost impossible victory over the British.

In the myth of the cherry tree, though, you can note something important: the mythical George Washington was not a general or the president of the United States when he took responsibility for cutting down his father's prized tree. He was a child.

There is a cliché: so easy that a child can do it. Guess what? It's no different when it comes to responsibility.

It's easy. So easy, in fact, that you can change the course of your life forever with five simple decisions.

Now that we've talked about Washington, let's talk about you. When you look in the mirror, what do you see? Do you see a responsible person? Do you see someone who is in control of your future?

Or do you see someone who is powerless, depressed, and suffering from circumstances that always seem out of control? Do you see someone who is unlucky?

Someone who can never catch a break? Someone who is unlucky in love or estranged from family and friends?

Are you that person who can never lose weight, build a business, get a promotion, meet someone special, get along with your family, or make lasting friendships?

You don't have to be that person. You don't want to be that person.

No book will help you if you don't take action. No therapist can fix what is wrong inside your heart unless you make the conscious decision to actively listen, be open-minded, and DO something. No person can make you happy unless you decide that you want to be happy.

Life is not a swimming pool. No one can save you if you're drowning in negative thinking, bad luck, or poor decisions. Only YOU can save you.

When I tell you this, I speak from firsthand experience. I went from a life of feeling suicidal and acting self-destructively to becoming a partner in a happy marriage, mother, bestselling author, and speaker on the national stage.

This didn't come from luck. I didn't wake up one morning and stumble onto a cool husband, happy child, book, and paid speaking schedule. I had to make a series of solid, actionable decisions before I could achieve any of these things.

Before I could really achieve or enjoy anything positive, I needed to take responsibility for my own happiness. I had to decide to live. I had to decide to be positive. I had to decide to work on my success. Most importantly, I had to decide that I was the ONLY person responsible for my own success and happiness. Luck has nothing to do with it.

Let's change things right now.

Here are the five decisions that will change your life forever.

Decision #1: Give yourself permission to be a responsible person.

This seems a little obvious, but it's the obvious things that we tend to overlook.

You have complete power to determine your success, happiness, and future. You just have to DECIDE that is what you want. No matter what you have told yourself in the past, you deserve to be happy. You deserve to have success.

You deserve to have a home life and career that are fulfilling and rewarding. To do that, you need to decide to let go of negative self-talk and open yourself to positive possibilities.

In the introduction of this book, I told you to set aside every self-help and business book you own. I said that NO book, therapy, plan, or class will help you unless you adopt the methods and strategies in this book. I am saying it again now.

Why? Unless you give yourself permission and make the conscious decision to take responsibility for your life, you will never be able to help yourself.

For some reason, we are wired to deny ourselves things that will make us happy. We instinctively believe that we do not deserve the very things we need to thrive and be successful. We have the power to change that old way of thinking. When we give ourselves permission, it trips the little wire in our brain, and suddenly, we CAN have and do the things we need to be happy.

I am not talking about giving yourself permission to eat a donut or to play hooky from work. Permission—when it comes to responsibility— is about being authentic and true. And when it works, you will feel it.

Let's start with a simple decision: losing weight. Eating better and exercising are the easiest things to forget or put aside in favor of ⁻omeone else's needs. They are also easy to forget and put aside ⁻ause we don't value our own needs. Then, when we try to diet, ⁱl because we have not given ourselves permission to be ⁱⁿ and succeed.

ⁿn of stress, failure, or conflict, we descend into ⁱk and eat and drink things that are bad for us. We ⁱ and allow others to sabotage us. We think we ⁱealthier or thinner. Why? We haven't made ⁱd given ourselves permission to eat better

ᶠor our success if we don't give ᶴful.

However, when you give yourself permission to be responsible, you give yourself that extra boost of authenticity. You are making a decision AND granting yourself permission to succeed.
Have you suffered a loss but have found that you can't grieve it? This loss can be a job, home, friendship, or even a loved one. Have you given yourself permission to grieve, or have you catered to everyone else's needs or internally told yourself that you don't have the right to mourn?

You can change that: give yourself permission to grieve. Say it aloud. Sit by yourself in a room, and tell yourself, "I give you permission to grieve." Wait. If you need to, say it again. Depending on the gravity of the loss, you might experience anything from a trickle to a flood of emotions. When you give yourself permission to truly feel, then you can begin the process of authentic healing. Otherwise, your pent-up sadness and grief will always get in the way.

Are you struggling with something at work but are stuck in frustration? Give yourself permission to be frustrated. Give yourself permission to not have all the answers. Give yourself permission to ask for help.

Give yourself permission to be imperfect because no one is perfect. The more you keep striving for perfection, the less likely you will be to embrace and learn from your mistakes.

Maybe you need to give yourself permission to be nicer to yourself. This has been a big one for me. I thought that, by being hard on myself, I would become successful, but I realized that I was my worst enemy. I had lost the ability to enjoy the process of things like writing books, learning a skill, or even being with my son.

59

It was a life-changing day when I sat down and told myself, "I give you permission to relax."

How do you start giving yourself permission to be responsible? Start with a mental inventory. Do you find yourself making excuses, falling into victimhood, being an enabler or being enabled, or simply stagnating because you haven't given yourself permission to succeed?

What are the stumbling blocks you have faced in life? Do they exist because you didn't give yourself permission to walk around them? Are there people in your life who have hurt, frustrated, belittled, or taken advantage of you and your kindness? Are you enabling anyone or being enabled? Give yourself permission to let go.

Keep the idea of permission in your head even if you can't think of anything now. (That's totally understandable. This book is full of information, and self-assessment takes time.)

es are that, as you open your eyes to the world of responsi-
will find places in your life that can be improved by one
ent of self-love: I give myself permission.

ecide to respond to life with love and

hared this book wondered why decision
successful, happy, or powerful. Yes,
efore you pursue those things, you
otives.

If your motives aren't good, your decisions will be meaningless, and you will ultimately fail.

What are your motives? Where do they come from? Do they come from a place of self-love? Or do they come from a place of bitterness? If they come from a place of jealousy, bitterness, revenge, or victimhood, you need to think about WHY you want to change.

Sure, we all have those moments when we say to ourselves, "I'll show him. I'll be a success, and he will come begging to me for money/forgiveness/my respect." But is that the philosophy and motive upon which you want to build your future? Can that truly make you happy?

People all around us are wildly successful and seem to have the world on a string. We see a lot of them on social media—taking pictures of themselves in faraway lands, enjoying the high life, and seeming to not have a care in the world.

Have you noticed, though, that some of those people—whose success is based on defeating others, destroying rivals, and seeking revenge on those who might have done them wrong in the past—seem to crash and burn, losing everything?

There is a simple reason: without a solid foundation based on empathy, love, and respect, any and all success is fleeting.

I challenge you to make the decision to enter your journey of taking responsibility from a place of love, empathy, and respect as you.

It won't be easy. You will have to bite your tongue, take deep breaths, count to five, and talk to yourself. (I have to all the time.) However, to truly take responsibility, you can't work from negative motives. Why? When you come from negative or nefarious motives, you are trying to control other people with your actions, and you can't control or take responsibility for the success, happiness, or failure of other people (even your adult children).

The only person you can take responsibility for is yourself, so if you come from a place of love, people will flock to you.

How do you decide to come from a place of love and empathy? You might need to completely realign your thinking.

Think about how public opinion has changed on once-taboo subjects because spokespeople for these causes came from a place of empathy. I spent 15 years in the movement to help adult survivors of childhood sexual abuse.

When I started this work, the general public was uncomfortable with the topic. They felt that, if we kept abuse victims quiet, the problem would eventually go away. The general public capitalized on the shame that victims feel. They were also embarrassed and ashamed themselves.

The victims, though, wouldn't stay silent, and it made many people uncomfortable.

In essence, many people thought that victims of sexual abuse were angry and hateful. They thought that our goal was to destroy institutions, such as the Catholic Church, Boy Scouts, and public schools. The reality, however, was far different.

We didn't come from a place of anger; we came from a place of fear—fear for children who might be at risk. We didn't demand that churches be destroyed or that churchgoers give up their faith; we asked that adults who abuse children be removed from ministry and held accountable according to the law. We also demanded that administrators who covered up crimes be held accountable.

Once the public saw the results of our work, and the abuse and cover-ups were exposed, public perception began to change.

If we had come from a place of anger or a desire to destroy the faith of innocent people, we never would have succeeded in protecting children and exposing crimes.

We came from a place of authentic empathy, and it worked. We exposed crimes, held wrongdoers accountable, and helped survivors heal. We also made generations of children safer from abuse.

The old saying is true: you attract more flies with honey than vinegar.

What happens if you don't come from a place of empathy and love? You might have short-term success, but can you ever be happy when your benchmark for success is other people's unhappiness or misfortune? If your plan for success comes from a place of revenge, do you think that you will attract people who want the best for you and lift you up? Will you be surrounded by people who help make you a better person? Will you be challenged to grow, emotionally and intellectually?

Probably not.

So check your motives. Good motives will serve you well for life as long as you act on them.

Decision #3: Being happy is a decision. Make it.

Do you want to be happy, so your children, friends, and family get to see and enjoy the authentic you? Do you want to leave the world a better place, just because you were there, helped people, made a difference, and were happy while you did it?

Do you want to be happy and successful because you have done the work, and you deserve it?

Yes. We all want to be happy. We all deserve to be happy. However, unless you make the decision to be happy, it will always be just beyond your grasp.

What good is your success if you aren't happy? Examples of empty success without happiness abound. Successful writers, business leaders, inventors, thinkers, and scientists have committed suicide because they could never get the one thing that eluded them: happiness.

Cleopatra, rocker Kurt Cobain, writers Sylvia Plath and Ernest Hemingway, code breaker and scientist Alan Turing, and actor Brian Keith are all examples of people who seemed to have it all, but they didn't. Happiness, acceptance, and love eluded them all.

You, however, don't have to be that way. You have the key to happiness: it's a decision.

When you see people who have fantastic career success, they will tell you that their family's happiness is their first priority. The most successful among them, including Tony Robbins and Oprah Winfrey, devote time every single day to meditation, visualization, or other things that bring them peace and happiness. They will tell you themselves: all the money in the world and the greatest career success are useless if they can't buy true friendship, companionship, or peace with yourself.

There are great books out there that will show you ways to find happiness. You can learn about meditation, mindfulness, and active listening. You can learn to let go, hang on, embrace, pull others close to you, or push away toxic people. You can get help for depression, addiction, and loss.

However, no book alone will do the job unless you change your mindset. All you need to do is decide.

If you are shocked by the idea, it's okay.

Through books, movies, families, and history, we have been led to believe that happiness is some kind of secret privilege bestowed on the wealthy and famous, the thin, the married, the single, the parent, the childless, the career woman, the stay-at-home mother, the religious, the atheist (notice the contradictions here).

The point is that we are taught that happiness is always just beyond our grasp. We are taught that, if we were just different or made different decisions, we could be happy.

Take a brief look at humankind and our history during the 20th and 21st centuries when people besides the very wealthy finally had the leisure time to think about happiness. The result? We are constantly on a quest for ever-elusive happiness.

We join clubs and churches, seek communities, meditate, pray, see therapists, visit communes, travel, enjoy sports, push our bodies, read, and search for answers to the ultimate question: how can I be happy?

We think that happiness is extrinsic, but it's not. It's inside ourselves as long as we make the decision to be happy. Happiness is a decision, and it's up to us to make it.

The only person who can make you happy is you. No other person will make you truly happy—they can add to your happiness, but they can't create it. No hobby, group, activity, or object, including money, will make you happy unless you decide to be happy and allow these things to add to your happiness.

In fact, happiness based on an object outside yourself (e.g., money, popularity, fame, accolades) is not really happiness—it's a false rush, like a drug. If you take the drug or the object away, the happiness evaporates and leaves a vacuum where you are even more miserable.

My decision to be happy was earth-shattering. I had been miserable for so long that sadness and depression were the only things I knew. Happiness was totally foreign. I thought it was a fantasy. As I became older and saw the results of my unhappiness (shame, self-destruction, failure, isolation), I thought that I deserved to be unhappy. I thought I was unworthy of feeling joy in the everyday like people around me.

As a literature major who spent her time reading the works of people who were wracked with depression and ultimately committed suicide, I began to believe that unhappiness was a badge of honor. I thought it made me smarter. I believed that happy people were dumb, uneducated, and naïve.

Pain and depression were my friends, and I took other people with me on the horrible journey. People who loved me tried to help me, but they could do nothing because I didn't think I was worthy of help.

It wasn't until my wake-up call that I could finally see myself from the outside. I saw that what I thought was intelligence and education was, in fact, delusion. I saw that I was hurting myself and the people who loved me. I was blind and missing the beauty of life.

When I realized that I was on a fast track to death—through my depression, self-destructive behaviors, self-sabotage, and isolation—I understood the decision I had to make. I wanted to live, so I had to decide to live AND thrive.

To do that, I had to decide to be happy.

Why? No one else could make that decision for me. No matter how much my friends loved me, they couldn't make the decision for me. My parents and sister could not change my course unless I made the decision. They could give me a hand to hold, but they could not save me.

There are no saviors. Only yourself.

Deciding to be happy is hard. You may have to break out of lifelong habits. You might have to re-train your face to smile and reorient your focus on the positive. You might have to jettison toxic people in your life.

You might have to eliminate stress, enjoy more fresh air, get off the computer, hug your children, or make amends with your parents. It might take 30 days of looking in the mirror and telling yourself that you are a happy person.

Once you get through the growing pains and make and act on your decision to be happy, though, you will never want to go back.

Decision #4: Make the decision to give up victimhood, and embrace your power.

Power is a funny thing.

Most crimes and ethical breaches are based on the abuse of power. Child sex abuse, for example, has nothing to do with sex at all. It's the abuse of power. Bullying is the same thing—abuse of power by an aggressor over someone weaker.

This decision is not about your power over other people, their motives, their actions, or their decisions. It is about your own internal power—your stamina, fortitude, and inner strength.

I am talking about victimhood—and your decision to kick it to the curb.

To be a responsible person, you have to embrace your inner power. You have to exercise power over your actions and your reactions to events and other people.

You have to have the fortitude to understand and deal with your emotions. You have to display stamina to change the way other people treat you.

You have to decide to no longer be a victim.

Victimhood can destroy you. Victims are the first to say that they have no control over their emotions and reactions. They let situations dominate their psyche. They expect other people to tread lightly around them. They have no self-control when handling the world around them and live in self-imposed fear, anger, sadness, shame, and isolation.

If you have ever heard of the terms "triggering" or "microaggressions," you are looking victimhood square in the face.

Being a victim stinks. I've been there. I let it control me. I relished it. It nearly killed me.

It's time to stop being a victim.

Happy, successful people who have inner power and embrace accomplishment are in control of their reactions. They don't bother wasting time being offended at innocuous remarks. They don't see slights in other people's political views. They don't take everything personally. They treat everyone as peers, not aggressors or enemies.

Successful and happy people are fair. They listen to and have compassion for other people's views. They don't waste time on people who focus only on other's faults and misdeeds. Instead, they devote their emotions to what is important: positive relationships.

Personal power is liberating and elevates us above the petty squabbles that surround us in our relationships, the Internet, politics, and other individual dogmas.

I spoke quite a bit about this in my TEDx talk. If you embrace your personal power, you can achieve ANYTHING. Why? You aren't wasting your time and energy on negative people, events, and feelings that you cannot change.

You can embrace power and control to focus on where you want to be instead of where you have been in the past.

It's easier than you think.

If you have trouble with triggers (situations or events that send you into an emotional tailspin), you have choices and can make these triggers disappear. Instead of surrendering and becoming a slave to events, decide to make a change for the better. See a therapist if that will help you.

Decide that you are more powerful than any book, story, idea, news event, movie, or person, and acknowledge that these things might arouse emotions in you. Then, tell yourself that you are powerful enough to let these feelings go before they take control.

The point is that you have to desensitize yourself to these triggers, or they will always be in control. You deserve to be free of them.

If the holidays upset you, create new holiday traditions. If spending time with your family distresses you, then make the decision to seek help with it. If dealing with your family is not a healthy option (especially in cases of addiction, abuse, or destructive behaviors), it's okay to let them go and create a new support system.

If you find that anger controls you, learn the power of forgiveness. Forgiveness is probably one of the most misunderstood and misused concepts in our society. It's not about forgetting your own or other people's transgressions. It's not about letting go of accountability. It's not about moving on so that a wrongdoer can continue to harm other people.

Rather, forgiveness is about letting go of anger that hurts you. It's about loving and caring for yourself. It's about finding accountability. It's about getting closure.

Simply put, forgiveness is the gift you give yourself.

Do you ever wonder why parents of murdered children eventually forgive the men or women who committed those crimes? It's because remaining angry does nothing positive. When these parents forgive, it doesn't mean that they want the murderers to go free. It doesn't mean that they don't want justice.

Rather, it means that they let go of the hurt and anger inside themselves—hurt and anger that keep them awake at night, destroy their lives, and damage all their relationships.

To embrace your personal power, you need to take a new view of forgiveness.

No one has ever achieved happiness or success by being a victim. No one ever created her future or wrote his own ending by embracing triggers or shouting about microaggressions. Those are victim behaviors that will keep you stuck and unhappy the rest of your life. They are regressive and only breed anger, pain, resentment, and discontent. It's impossible to be happy if you remain a victim. Period.

If you are ready to decide that you are powerful, it's time to kiss victimhood goodbye.

You need to have power over your body. You can have power over your thinking.

You can't change your past, but you can have power over your NOW and your future.

Take a minute to absorb that.

Did you know that you have power over the way other people treat you? Yes. You have power over your personal and emotional boundaries. You have the power to stop people from taking advantage of you, shaming you, or doing anything else that violates you. You have the power to smile in the face of adversity. You have power over how you handle yourself and allow other people to interact with you.

You are a powerful person if you decide to be, so act like one. Hold your head high. Speak with authority. Smile like you mean it.

Being powerful does not mean that you are aggressive. It does not mean that you are loud or dominant. Rather, you are comfortable and confident in your skin. It means that people know that you have strong boundaries, stand up for yourself, and won't be pushed around. You are quick with a smile and do your best to be positive.

People are attracted to you because of this confidence and want to help you achieve your goals.

Don't worry if you are shy or introverted—personal power and confidence are just as important and effective for people who, like me, struggle daily with introversion as they are for aspiring politicians. Positive personal power comes hand in hand with love and empathy, so you will soon find yourself surrounded by exciting, engaged, caring, and passionate people.

Personal power is a people magnet, and once you decide that you are powerful, your new friendships will amaze you. Your ability to make good decisions and fulfill promises will increase because you will enter situations with the confidence and the personal power to do what you need to succeed.

Do you struggle with self-esteem and confidence issues? Then personal power is your new friend. It's a steppingstone toward self-confidence and self-esteem. When you assert power, shed powerlessness, and continue to do so habitually, self-confidence is the result.

Once you find that you have personal power and confidence, it's far easier to believe and say, "I am a worthwhile person, deserving of good things!"

Like happiness, being powerful might also be a tough philosophy to adopt at first, and like all good habits, it takes practice.

Decision #5: Decide to create your future and limitless success.

No one else can determine your future. Your boss, spouse, children, parents, friends, past—we now know that these people have absolutely no power or influence over your future. Sure, they might influence situations, but that's not your future. Situations are just events that might or might not happen.

Your future and your success are what YOU create. And the only person who can hijack or destroy your future is … you.

My TEDx talk discussed this topic in detail, including how much personal power and time we waste on scapegoats.

We love scapegoats. They make life easier for us because we don't have to take responsibility or blame for any of the bad things that happen—such as our career and personal failures.

It's easy to blame other people for our shortfalls. In fact, the human condition is one of finger-pointing and embracing the "not me!" philosophy. Think about the people we blame the most when we fail or suffer as adults. The number one target? Our parents.

We LOVE to blame our parents for the reasons that our lives are messed up. It's so easy to blame an overprotective mother for our career failures or a domineering father for our rising debt.

It's our divorced parents' fault that we can't find love. It's our father's alcoholism that drove us to use drugs well into our 30s.

Blame. Blame. Blame. Why? It's easy, and we don't have to take responsibility for our actions.

I am very familiar with parental blame. In this book and my TEDx talk, I have referred to my mother's alcoholism and my father's denial. As they struggled with their own issues and were inattentive toward me, a child-sex predator was able to worm his way into my life and change it forever.

For years after the abuse, it was very easy to blame my parents. It was easy to say that it was their fault I was hurting and depressed. It was easy to say that it was their fault that I was sexually promiscuous. It was easy to blame them for my nonexistent career. It was easier to blame them than it was to fix the problem because by this time, the problem wasn't they; it was I.

By the time I was 25, every decision I had made since age 18 was mine, not theirs. It was my decision to not get help for my depression. It was my decision to act out sexually instead of talking to a therapist to get to the root of the problem. It was my decision to make self-sabotaging choices that cost me jobs.

Those were all my decisions, not theirs.

In fact, by the time I was 27, I came to a shocking realization: my parents had done their job. I went to great schools and graduated from college. They were loving. They cared about my well-being.

I was clothed and fed and allowed to travel and study in Europe for a year. They paid my bills through college. When I was sick, they nursed me until I was well.

Was it their fault I was sexually abused? No. It was my abuser's fault. To this day, my father would do or give anything to change what happened. My abuse was not my parents' fault. It was my abuser's fault.

It was time to stop blaming them for how I had chosen to live my life after the abuse.

They loved me and did a great job. Were they perfect? No. And neither was I.

My future was mine to create or destroy. My parents had nothing to do with it. It was time to forgive them and time to change my life.

When you decide to create your future, you have to let go of past anger, regret, and blame. You have to let go of your past (unless it is a positive motivator for you!) and tell yourself that you are worthy of the best future ever.

Now that we've forgiven our parents, let's talk about other people who we give way too much power over our future: our bosses, jobs, and colleagues at work.

Your boss has an agenda and a list of priorities, as any good boss should. Your boss most likely has set one-, five-, and 10-year goals for herself, the division, and the company.

However, your boss isn't in charge of seeking, setting, or achieving your goals. She isn't in charge of creating your dreams, envisioning your future, or writing your ending. That's up to you.

Your boss and colleagues might deal you setbacks, but the only person who can really destroy your career and your future is you. It's not their job to make you happy or unleash your potential. That's up to you.

Your limitless success relies on one factor: you.

Only you can create authentic goals for yourself. Only you can encourage your boss, colleagues, and direct reports to help you achieve those goals. Only you can walk into work with a smile on your face and the willingness to get the job done.

Only you can strive to be a better, happier, more successful person who changes the world and seizes success.

See how it's all coming together?

Nobody lies on his deathbed and says, "I should have worked more hours." Many people, though, lay there and think, "Why did I let other people convince me that my dreams and goals weren't worthwhile?"

No workplace is perfect, but if you find that you are in a mentally and emotionally unhealthy situation, it's time to take the responsibility to find a new path. If you are fired, it's time to take responsibility and find a different path.

If you are laid off, it's time to take responsibility and forge your own path. You might fail sometimes, but if you don't take responsibility and try, you will never succeed.

What does creating your future look like? Is it a career change? Do you want more education? Does your future include building a family? Founding a company? All of these things? What is success to you? Is it financial? Spiritual? Emotional?

Write it down, and make it happen. Take responsibility for creating the future that you want.

In 1997, I was laid off from a job and freshly divorced, and found myself waiting tables despite a college degree and graduate work. It wasn't where I wanted to be. Sure, my shifts were fun, and I met wonderful people, but I couldn't pay the bills or do many of the things I wanted to do. I felt like a failure.

However, the only person who could take responsibility and pull me up was I.

It was time to make a change and create the future I wanted. For me, it took a move, asking for help, and lots of hard work. Soon, I was in a good job in my career field (public relations at the time). Although that was what I needed, it was only a first step.

I wanted to do great things, make a difference, and challenge myself to make the world a better place. To do that, though, I had to take action.

After two more years, I was in a better job with more responsibilities, higher pay, and increased opportunities. It wasn't a smooth road, but I rose to the challenge and did the best work that I could.

Until I was laid off one Friday afternoon.

That was a devastating blow. Whether you lose a job due to downsizing or your performance, it affects your self-esteem. I felt worthless, used, angry, scared, and betrayed. I had held up my end of the bargain with my employer, so why didn't it do the same for me? I did my fair share of crying. I yelled. I shouted. I ranted to my soon-to-be husband. I called my dad for sympathy.

After a weekend of anger and self-pity, however, I had to move on. I had bills to pay and other financial obligations. I didn't have time to feel sorry for myself. Sure, I was still angry. Of course, I felt betrayed. However, those feelings weren't going to help me get a job, so on the Sunday night after the layoff, I had to make a plan—my plan.

Instead of seeing the layoff as a blow to my career, I realized that it was the best thing that had happened to me. I had always wanted to work for myself, but I never had the nerve to make the leap. I hated the corporate atmosphere, but I was too insecure to trade it in for the uncertainty of becoming a freelancer.

To be honest, I hated being told what to do. I was sick of working on projects in which I didn't believe and working for people who were not always honest about their products. I wanted to pick and choose my work. I wanted to be in charge.

I began to write my future. I wrote down on what I wanted to work and how I wanted to work. I began reaching out to people who could help me. I began networking.

And the work started to come in.

Like all things, though, this work was a process. I had to experiment with what I liked and what I didn't. I took some projects and turned down others. Some I liked, and some I didn't. They were all my projects, and their success or failure depended on me.

A few years later, I went forward publicly about my sexual abuse. A new law allowed me to use the civil courts to expose my abuser and the cover-up of my abuse by high school administrators.

As a result, the freelance work dried up. I was on the news and the front page of the paper—and clergy sexual abuse was still a very taboo subject—so my clients stopped sending me projects. When your job it to be a publicist, it's not a great strategy to be the topic of the 6 o'clock news yourself.

I faced with another choice. I could tone down my activism and keep my work, but that wasn't what I wanted. I was passionate about my activism. I loved helping other survivors, exposing abuse, and making sure wrongdoers were held accountable.

It was time to rewrite my future, so I did. This time, I made my activism and advocacy my career, and I loved it.

As of this writing, it has been 12 years since I made that decision, and even now, I am constantly rewriting my future the way I want it to be. When I do, I become more successful. I create a better, more exciting, and more financially rewarding future every time.

You can do anything and create any future you want. If a survivor of childhood sexual abuse (who struggled with lifelong depression, an alcoholic parent, divorce, layoffs, and publicity about her less-than-stellar life) can do it, you can.

You just have to give yourself permission to be happy, embrace the power within you, take responsibility for the process and the outcomes, and create the future that YOU want.

For you, creating your future might involve writing down goals. It might be sitting with your spouse and asking her to listen and not interrupt or judge while you talk about your dreams. It might be finally talking to your friend about your great business idea.

The only person who can stop you or hold you back is you.

You don't even have to be specific about creating your future. In 1997, I never thought that, by 2015, I would be making money writing books and speaking. I did know, though, that I deserved to be happy and that I was capable of the work required to fulfill my dreams.

In 2003, I didn't know that I would have a beautiful son and truly embrace motherhood and everything that goes with it, but I knew that I wanted to write a future where I was surrounded with love.

You won't always succeed. In fact, you are doomed to fail at least once. If you don't fail, how will you know success? If you don't fail, how will you learn? If you don't fail, how will you ever know that your passion and dreams are worthwhile? From now on, though, failure will not have power over you.

In fact, if you do fail, you're in good company.

Babe Ruth had the record for most strikeouts during his career.

The creators of the ubiquitous lubricant and protectant WD40 failed 39 times before they found the right formula.

Milton Hershey started (and lost) three candy companies before founding Hershey. He didn't even get into the candy business until after he was fired from a job as a printer.

Arianna Huffington, founder of the *Huffington Post*, was turned down by 36 publishers. Sixteen publishers and an agent rejected John Grisham. Every publishing house that saw my books turned me down, but I didn't let that stop me. The fact that you are reading this book tells me that my instincts were right!

Expect to fail. Embrace it, learn from it, grow from it, move on, and succeed.

Your future is yours to write. Your success is yours to define and create.

You just have to make the decision and take action.

Five decisions. Five choices. Millions of ways to change your life for the better.

But there is one more decision you have to make.

CHAPTER SEVEN

THE FINAL DECISION

The book is short, but your task is long: it's time to take responsibility for your life. I've shown you that it is within your power to shed your emotional crutches.

You have the ability and strength to let go of victimhood. You have inner power. You can create your future. You can create your success.

Now it's time to do the work.

In the introduction, I told you to put down any other self-help book you're reading until you have finished this book. I told you to shove aside diet books, career books, and books about finding happiness or inner peace.

Decision #6: Decide to take action.

Now that you've made it this far, you know why: the best plan in the world will never work unless you make the conscious decision to take action. You have to decide to be happy and successful and to have the future or career that you want before any self-help book makes a dent.

So now what?

Here is your assignment: go back and look over the first five decisions. You might need to re-read the entire section to absorb the importance of each decision. What do you want to accomplish?

Who do you want to be? How do you want to feel while you are on your journey? What kind of people do you want to attract?

After you have looked over the previous chapter and thought about your decisions, it's time to get a piece of paper and a pen. When you are ready, write down these statements:

> I give myself permission to be a responsible person.
> I have decided to respond with love and empathy.
> I have decided to be happy.
> I have decided to give up victimhood and embrace my personal power.
> I have decided to create my future and unlimited success.

You can phrase the statements in the way that works best for you. I have found that the phrases "give myself permission" or "made the decision" are the most effective for myself.

Now, take out another piece of paper. On this sheet, write the following:

> I am a responsible person.
> I respond to people and situations with love and empathy.
> I am happy.
> I have given up victimhood, and I embrace my personal power.
> I create my future and my unlimited success.

Now that you have completed both sheets, put the second sheet on your bedside table. These are your affirmations. You will return to the first sheet in a moment.

First thing in the morning, take out that sheet, and read it. If you feel comfortable doing so, read it aloud. (This might seem a little uncomfortable at first, but the more you do it, the more you will see its effectiveness.)

Reading these affirmations in your own handwriting with your own voice every day will not only cement the new life you are creating for yourself but also give you confidence, self-esteem, and needed encouragement from your biggest fan (that's you!).

As with all good habits, it will take you about 21 days to make this exercise a solid part of your routine. I invite you to take responsibility to do just that. It's easy, it's fast, it's simple—and it will change your life.

Affirmations like these are very powerful. Successful people worldwide have used them to build impactful, financially lucrative careers. In interviews, people, such as Oprah Winfrey, motivational powerhouse Tony Robbins, and even actor Jim Carrey, have used affirmations and visualizations to chart their course for success.

What about the first sheet? That's your back-up. Making the decision to change your life is hard. You will have down days. You will come home frustrated, angry, and feeling like a failure. On those days, reading affirmations might just make your mood worse.

When you feel down, I want you to pull out the first sheet. Keep it somewhere safe and accessible, so you can get to it when you need it.

The beauty of decisions is that, when you want to give up and go back to your old ways of living, you can make these decisions again. You can reaffirm your commitment to yourself. Married people renew their vows all of the time, so why shouldn't you renew your vows to yourself—especially when you need them the most? Reaffirm your decisions.

Reaffirm that you have decided to take action. Tell yourself that it's okay to stumble and fail; otherwise, you never learn how to stand tall and succeed.

The only person who can assume this responsibility is you. And you're worthy.

So get to work.

CONCLUSION

Life is full of magic and joy. Unfortunately, many of us have lost the way.

Whoever made up the story about George Washington and the cherry tree was no dummy. That person knew that teaching about responsibility in the context of a children's story would tell the youngest among us about the importance of responsibility in our own lives.

That's why we strive to teach our children moral values early in life. We want them to have empathy, compassion, inner strength, honesty, and other values that will help them become strong, contributing members of society.

We want them to appreciate the value of hard work, education, the beauty of nature, and the infinite opportunities humankind has to better the world and other people.

Sometimes, however, we lose the way. It's not anyone's fault; it's just something that happens. Life circumstances, tragedy, loss, setbacks, frustration, and shame lure us off the path of happiness and success by coaxing us into giving up responsibility and feeling powerless over ourselves.

The purpose of this book—and my TEDx talk—is to change that. By making the five decisions I have outlined and by taking responsibility for your life, you can recapture the magic that is excitement.

You can take back your dreams and make them happen. You can find the joy in the simple, little things in life because you have decided that happiness is yours for the taking.

I'll close this book with the same statement as the opening. Now, you understand its power.

> *It doesn't matter who you were yesterday. It doesn't matter who you were five minutes ago. The only things that matter are who you are right now and the kind of person you decide to be from this moment onward.*

You will have a future that you create, and you will experience success without limits. All you have to do is decide to do so.

You are unstoppable. And now, you are free to soar.

ACKNOWLEDGEMENTS

Thank you to my family, my friends, and the amazing people behind TEDxPasadenaWomen, especially Amber Nelson.

And to Chandler, Emily, Omer, Sean, and Chelsea at SPS.

ABOUT THE AUTHOR

Joelle Casteix is an author, speaker, and leading national "in the trenches" expert on the prevention and exposure of child sex abuse and cover-up.

Her TEDx talk on the power of responsibility quickly went viral, making her an in-demand corporate, university and motivational speaker. She has inspired thousands with her stores of hope, action, and the power of her "Six Decisions."

Visit **www.Casteix.com**

While there, you can watch the video, gain special access to exclusive free books and materials, and find out when Joelle will be speaking in your area.

15244280R00059

Printed in Great Britain
by Amazon.co.uk, Ltd.,
Marston Gate.